FULLER INSPIRATIONS

Daily Affirmations to Think Positively and Live Positively

WADIAH FULLER

Fuller Inspirations: Daily Affirmations to Think Positively and Live Positively

Copyright © 2021 by Wadiah Fuller

LCCN: 2020922717

ISBN: 978-1-7361529-0-4 (print)

ISBN: 978-1-7361529-1-1 (ebook)

The information in this book is meant to supplement, not replace, the medical/ mental health advice of physicians and/or therapists. The reader should regularly consult a physician and/or therapists in matters relating to his/her mental health and particularly with respect to any symptoms that may require diagnosis or medical attention.

Printed in the United States of America

DEDICATION

This book is dedicated to my amazing daughter, Naysa Sabriya.
May you always be inspired from within to be Great!

THANK YOU

I would like to Thank God for not only inspiring me to write this book, but providing me with the wisdom and words to complete a project in which I could never take full credit.

Thank you to my parents for always supporting me. Thank you to my siblings for providing me with my most insightful self-reflection.

The Conversation

Look, I'm not trying to start conflict
But I think it's time that we talk
Last night these thoughts were rolling thru my head
As I went on my evening walk

And before you interrupt me
I just want you to hear me out
It seems that every time I try to better myself
You just sit over there and pout

You're rolling your eyes and shaking your head
As if I don't have a clue
Looking at me with a puzzled face
Asking if I'm "sure that's what I want to do"

You make comments about my inadequacies
As if they define who I am
Sure, I have room to grow
But you treat every step like it's an exam

You're supposed to be my number one supporter
The person I could always look to
But when I start working on my dreams
You have the audacity to say, "Nah, you ain't gonna be able to do that Boo!"

These things have been going on for years
And I wish you could be on my team
Even though you're the closest to me
You act like you hope I fail, it seems

I'm 'bout ready to have you see me
Because Enough is Enough
Don't you know that even without ALL of your comments
Life is still Tough

I admit, I really value your opinion
But I'm tired of your constant critique
I would dismiss you from my life
But YOU are actually ME

By
Wadiah Fuller

INTRODUCTION

Is there something inside of you calling you to greatness? Do you constantly find yourself in search of the true meaning of life and your life's purpose? This is not a book that has all the answers that you have been seeking. Although, it is a book that will provide you with the direction in which to walk towards. Spoiler alert! As you read this book daily, you will learn two things: 1) "What you seek, you already are" (Deepak Chopra); 2) "What you seek, is seeking you" (Rumi). This book is designed to not only read from beginning to end. Rather, it is meant to be read continuously, as it will inspire you throughout the day and throughout your life.

The word *inspiration*, according to Merriam-Webster, derives from the Latin root word *inspiratus* which means to "breathe into"/ "to breathe life into" or referring to "having divine influence from a divine source." Do you believe words can breathe life into you? Similar to the way we encourage a baby to walk by saying, "Come on, you can do it!" We continue to give them inspiring words of hope, knowing they will fall again. But as you get older, who gives you hope? What are the words you say to yourself? Are they encouraging, or do you set limits?

In the spring of 2018, I was in search of inspiration. I felt as if I was living the same day over and over with no real progress. It didn't help that the last major goal I'd accomplished was 15 years prior when I completed my Master's in Social Work. Daily, I was struggling to arrive to work on time despite the hope of making a change. When it came to my personal goal of writing a book, I would start, then it would get shelved. This process happened several times. While speaking to a friend about my concerns, she expressed the same. In an effort to move past the rut we were both in, we decided to start our mornings with an affirmation. I love affirmations! Each time I read one, I drift into my own thoughts, deciphering what it means to me and how I can achieve the goal of really feeling and believing the affirmation is present in my life. Yes, sometimes I can be my own worst critic. However, actually believing the words I say, means identifying practical steps needed to make that affirmation true for me. Soon, summer arrived. As I don't work during the summers, I no longer needed to get to work on time, so our morning conferences ceased. Nevertheless, the power of saying daily affirmations stayed with me, but I continued to ponder what they meant and what the steps are to reach the goal of the affirmation. Thus, the idea to create affirmations that bridge the gap between desire and reality came into fruition.

Affirmations are positive statements you say to yourself to build self-confidence. They should be written in the present tense. The power of affirmations comes from succumbing to the feeling of what that experience would be like. Repeat the affirming words to yourself quietly or aloud throughout the day. The more you repeat the positive words, the more they become a part of the fabric of who you are. Muhammad Ali, one of the greatest boxers of all time, stated, "It is the repetition of affirmations that leads to belief. And once that belief becomes a deep conviction, things began to happen."

It is important to note that it is quite difficult to control your thoughts. Negative thoughts can occur due to the impact of our life experiences that can include trauma, hurtful situations, disappointment and among other things. The act of changing your thoughts is a daily practice. Even if you don't believe it now, say it anyway. If the affirmation doesn't feel good when you say it, challenge yourself to confront your negative feeling/thought. What belief do you have about yourself or the world that is holding you back from greatness? Part of changing your thoughts requires honesty (with yourself) about your current beliefs about you. Take some time to sit alone and reflect on how you really feel. What areas of your life do you need to improve? Have you ever given yourself enough time and space to really think about this? And how can you make it better? Lastly, which step are you starting today? Although, I firmly believe in affirmations, one must also take action. Even if the progress is a small step, it is important to take ownership of our lives and move towards our goals.

This book was written for those who, not only want to be inspired, but who want to go straight into action with a step-by-step daily practice. Each affirmation is written with a unique and practical way of achieving your goal. Let's proceed with this journey together.

References: Chopra, Deepak. 2004. *The Book of Secrets: Unlocking the Hidden Dimensions of Your Life*. Penguin Random House Publishing. (Quoted in Introduction).

How To Use This Book

SAY AN AFFIRMATION DAILY (by using one of the following methods)

- Follow along from Day 1 thru Day 365.

- Choose randomly.

- Choose one affirmation that you say daily for the entire week

SAY IT WITH EMOTION

- Stand up straight, say the affirmation aloud and say each affirmation with the same emotion as if it already exists in your life.

SAY IT REPETITIVELY

- Repeat your chosen affirmation throughout the day.

- Write the affirmation down and post it where you can see it during the day.

DAY 1

I am Thankful for the lessons
I am Thankful for the guidance
I am Thankful for the solitude
I am Thankful for the alliance

Fuller Inspirations

DAY 2

I overcome challenges
Any fears, I always face
I learn from what life gives me
My growth, I choose to embrace

Fuller Inspirations

DAY 3

I accept life's Blessings
I feel them all around me
I move as if I have them
Floating high and living freely

Fuller Inspirations

DAY 4

I am open to new opportunities
My life is full of growth
I receive happiness and success
Believe me, I can have them both

Fuller Inspirations

DAY 5

I will
I always reach my goal
I know without doubt
I feel it in my mind, heart and soul

Fuller Inspirations

DAY 6

I am so thankful for all things
My life is truly Blessed
Although, I've lived thru ups and downs
This life of mine is the Best

Fuller Inspirations

DAY 7

I am a Superhero
I stand tall and save the day
I plan for my successes
I'm known to find a way

Fuller Inspirations

DAY 8

This is my life
And I choose how it is to be
I work hard on my plans
So the fruits of my labor, I do see

Fuller Inspirations

DAY 9

My future self
Will forever be Super pleased
I always push past tough moments
Despite the lack of ease

Fuller Inspirations

DAY 10

My glass is half full
My heart is overflowing with love
I can achieve all things
While staying a step above

Fuller Inspirations

DAY 11

I am Bold
I always make it work
I look fear in the eye
And step forward with a smirk

Fuller Inspirations

DAY 12

Dear self
Know that you are loved beyond measure
I own who I am
And every day I say, "I am a Treasure!"

Fuller Inspirations

DAY 13

I am healthy and vibrant
My soul is full of peace
I keep my thoughts positive
Accepting life's increase

Fuller Inspirations

DAY 14

I have plenty of talents
I do whatever I choose
With perseverance and hard work
All winners leave these clues

Fuller Inspirations

DAY 15

Despite the hardships

I always push past the pain

Even a kid knows

Before the Rainbow, there is rain

Fuller Inspirations

DAY 16

There have been mistakes
My past has helped me grow
I pay attention to the lessons
Therefore, the farther I go

Fuller Inspirations

DAY 17

I choose happiness
And I experience many Great things
Each day I smile
As I am excited about what life brings

Fuller Inspirations

DAY 18

I was made to create change
I make the world a better place
I transform the current situation
Using my vision to improve each case

Fuller Inspirations

DAY 19

I am Gorgeous
My inner beauty gives a Glow
I walk tall with pride
Even with silence, they want to see my flow

Fuller Inspirations

DAY 20

Why worry about the future
When I decide what I want to do
With each step that I take
I triumphantly push thru

Fuller Inspirations

DAY 21

Forgiveness is a choice
It is the way to happiness and peace
To achieve these things
I choose first to forgive me

Fuller Inspirations

DAY 22

Challenges will come
It's about how I proceed
I am continuously moving forward
Executing everything I need

Fuller Inspirations

DAY 23

My habits are my choices
To create them, they say 21 days
Each day, I choose purposefully
And it is my Good habit that stays

Fuller Inspirations

DAY 24

I am confident in myself
My imperfections make me Unique
I show Self love and love for others
Both thru my actions and when I speak

Fuller Inspirations

DAY 25

I am Grateful for all things
I believe my life is by design
Even if I thought I didn't want it
I know all my experiences are divine

Fuller Inspirations

DAY 26

Although things can be difficult
Just know I will never quit
I make improvements everyday
Every trial is to my benefit

Fuller Inspirations

DAY 27

I choose to make things happen
Excuses are for the weak
Everyday I work harder and wiser
Always striving to reach my peak

Fuller Inspirations

DAY 28

I look fear in the eye
To do it anyway is to be brave
I continue to prevail
A road of tenacity, I always pave

Fuller Inspirations

DAY 29

I accept life for what it is
Letting go of what could be
Living in the moment right now
Able to see all of life's beauty

Fuller Inspirations

DAY 30

My thoughts, I can control
They dictate the direction of my journey
I stay focused on improving
Only positive thoughts come from me

Fuller Inspirations

DAY 31

I sit still and calm my body
And with my mind, I embrace peace
Taking each breath slowly
All negativity, I release

Fuller Inspirations

DAY 32

I am in harmony with the world
I stay centered by showing gratitude
Peace and blessings I wish to all
I strive daily to elevate the mood

Fuller Inspirations

DAY 33

This world is Abundant
There is more than enough for us all
With limitless dreams
On all my successes, I stand tall

Fuller Inspirations

DAY 34

I release all self-doubt
My life is exactly how it should be
Mixed with some good and some bad
These moments have paved the path for me

Fuller Inspirations

DAY 35

Love is all around me
I feel it in everything I do
I unconditionally love myself
And without judgement, I love you

Fuller Inspirations

DAY 36

Today I plant my seeds
So tomorrow my flowers will grow
I water the spot daily
Providing consistency not just hope

Fuller Inspirations

DAY 37

My obstacles are never too big
It's all about my perception
I overcome any and every setback
Even before the thought of its inception

Fuller Inspirations

DAY 38

I honor this life
My worth is more than what I gain
I believe in me
Everything I need, I already contain

Fuller Inspirations

DAY 39

I am always patient
What is for me, will come to me
It may not come right now
But it's mine, I guarantee

Fuller Inspirations

DAY 40

I am my own competition
To compare to others is wasted time
I improve myself everyday
The only score I have to beat is mine

Fuller Inspirations

DAY 41

I Love myself
There is no one like me
I can achieve anything
I work hard on my dream

Fuller Inspirations

DAY 42

I have always been different
My differences are what make me Great
I embrace all of who I am
To succeed in this life is my Fate

Fuller Inspirations

DAY 43

I look within to find my treasure
To focus on others distracts my vision
I meditate daily to lift my thoughts
Awakened by the clarity of my decision

Fuller Inspirations

DAY 44

I remain steadfast
My goals, I do complete
I move forward daily
Needing growth like I need to eat

Fuller Inspirations

DAY 45

I make my intentions daily
And plan the life that I want for me
I think it and put it into action
All of what I want, has come to be

Fuller Inspirations

DAY 46

I am confident in my choices
I only need approval from me
I weigh out all the pros and cons
Keeping a cool and level head is key

Fuller Inspirations

DAY 47

I am organized with all my tasks
Doing a little with each passing day
I am determined to reach my goal
Unwavering consistency is the way

Fuller Inspirations

DAY 48

I am great in all I do
Even my failures help me excel
I continue to keep moving
Using life's lessons to make me prevail

Fuller Inspirations

DAY 49

I am present in the moment
I forgive myself for past mistakes
I release anxieties about my future
Focusing on the now is what it takes

Fuller Inspirations

DAY 50

I stay eager to learn
Exploring all that I can
I listen more than I talk
Understanding is the plan

Fuller Inspirations

DAY 51

I am my biggest fan
Each day, I roll out the Red Carpet
I applaud all of my successes
Anything I want, I go get it

Fuller Inspirations

DAY 52

Even the impossible is possible
I have faith in all that I do
I believe anything can happen
I know all my dreams come true

Fuller Inspirations

DAY 53

I can do anything
Limitations never hold me back
I work harder and longer
Winning for me is a fact

Fuller Inspirations

DAY 54

I am fulfilling my purpose
My dreams are here to stay
I am relentless in moving forward
By any means, I'll find a way

Fuller Inspirations

DAY 55

I have genuine connections with others
I can trust them with my heart
I surround myself with positive people
We respect each other from the start

Fuller Inspirations

DAY 56

Changes will come
I encourage them and expect growth
I welcome each change as my teacher
From now on, this is my oath

Fuller Inspirations

DAY 57

I am Whole
I seek my answers from within
I bring 100 percent every time
Knowing I always seem to win

Fuller Inspirations

DAY 58

I accept the timeline of my life
It's okay that I have a different journey
Each step moves me to my purpose
There is never a need to hurry

Fuller Inspirations

DAY 59

I am capable
I take time to learn what I don't know
I improve daily
Watch and see how far I'll go

Fuller Inspirations

DAY 60

I am happy for your success
I know we can all get what we desire
I applaud all my sisters and brothers
I am proud of all that you acquire

Fuller Inspirations

DAY 61

I move from my comfort zone
I choose to be great
I want more than good enough
I start on this date

Fuller Inspirations

DAY 62

I am a Star
My light shines in the dark
I do what it takes
And I always hit my mark

Fuller Inspirations

DAY 63

I always succeed
Only because I believe that I can
The actions I take
Are sure to make winning the plan

Fuller Inspirations

DAY 64

I treat myself with respect
So that others will follow my lead
Keeping my head held high
Saying, "I am Great!" is my creed

Fuller Inspirations

DAY 65

Even if you never know
I forgive you for all you've done
My heart heals as I release
Letting go of negativity is how I won

Fuller Inspirations

DAY 66

I can say "No" without guilt
And still pray for your success
Because I do right by me
Doesn't mean I value you any less

Fuller Inspirations

DAY 67

I ask for what I want
And have Faith I will receive
My belief is boundless
Anything I want I do achieve

Fuller Inspirations

DAY 68

I see Greatness in my vision
This is how it becomes my reality
Putting forth all my effort
Produces positive outcomes, I guarantee

Fuller Inspirations

DAY 69

I earn all my successes
Nothing I do is by chance
My dedication is the answer
Along with hard work, I advance

Fuller Inspirations

DAY 70

I am healed from past traumas
I acknowledge them and speak my truth
I grow wiser and stronger
As I release the chains from my youth

Fuller Inspirations

DAY 71

I stay grinding on my plans
My momentum keeps a steady flow
Putting in work on a regular
My results constantly grow

Fuller Inspirations

DAY 72

I have the right to change my mind
When others judge, I feel free
My choices are all my own
My inner circle lets me be me

Fuller Inspirations

DAY 73

I am understanding of what chose to leave
Knowing that better is on its way
I see lessons in that loss
Trust me I'm more than okay

Fuller Inspirations

DAY 74

My circle is Great
I stay amongst the Best
We encourage each other
Living a life that's Blessed

Fuller Inspirations

DAY 75

I celebrate my life
And all the accomplishments that arise
I visualize success now
And I walk the walk to the prize

Fuller Inspirations

DAY 76

What happens in my life
Is a mirror of what I think
I choose to think positively
So that my thoughts and actions link

Fuller Inspirations

DAY 77

Dear Self
I love you as you are
I am Thankful for my body
It's more than up to par

Fuller Inspirations

DAY 78

I believe in miracles
My doubts only set me back
I know in my heart it's coming
With Faith like this, I stay on track

Fuller Inspirations

DAY 79

I approach life with confidence
Leaving fear on the sideline
Shouting out, "I got this!"
And saying, "The world is mine!"

Fuller Inspirations

DAY 80

As I look in the mirror
I know that I am Grand
I was flawlessly created
Every room I enter, I command

Fuller Inspirations

DAY 81

My life has a rhythmic flow
I experience what's up and what's down
Never living too long in either
I stay steady when wearing my crown

Fuller Inspirations

DAY 82

Each day is a new beginning
I have the power to improve me
I can do better than yesterday
My success is my responsibility

Fuller Inspirations

DAY 83

I give this life my all
Winning is the only choice
I leave myself no options
Everyone will hear my voice

Fuller Inspirations

DAY 84

I have an Amazing family
I am building for many generations
Our Greatness is our Legacy
You can see this in all my operations

Fuller Inspirations

DAY 85

I embrace this Great Love
One that makes me feel complete
With Ever-Lasting devotion
That kind of Love, I give to me

Fuller Inspirations

DAY 86

I am in Harmony
My thoughts and actions are one
I do what I know is right
I keep going until it's done

Fuller Inspirations

DAY 87

I am healthy
In my body, my spirit and my mind
I take care of me
And always treat myself kind

Fuller Inspirations

DAY 88

I am more than a "Realist"
I envision what I want for me
I make changes in my life
I am living my Fantasy

Fuller Inspirations

DAY 89

My thoughts are valued
Others marvel in what I say
My voice is always heard
Having confidence is the way

Fuller Inspirations

DAY 90

I am always on time
I prepare in advance
The moves that I make
Are never left to chance

Fuller Inspirations

DAY 91

I sit patiently
I allow insight to enter
I am open to new things
The world is my mentor

Fuller Inspirations

DAY 92

I am gifted
I wisely use my resources
I make things happen
Despite the outside forces

Fuller Inspirations

DAY 93

I listen carefully

There are lessons all around me

I learn from others' mistakes

My growth also comes from what I see

Fuller Inspirations

DAY 94

I trust my decisions
Even if I fail, I never lose
I'm constantly taking steps
Staying on the path that I choose

Fuller Inspirations

DAY 95

I speak positively about me
I love how I've grown
I block all outside comments
I stay in my positive zone

Fuller Inspirations

DAY 96

I give freely
My smile can lift a nation
I am helpful to others
I give their success a standing ovation

Fuller Inspirations

DAY 97

I start fresh today
My dreams, I put in place
I keep pushing
Meeting my goal is always the case

Fuller Inspirations

DAY 98

I can do it
I let go of the doubt
I hold on to my Faith
And keep the fear out

Fuller Inspirations

DAY 99

I know my purpose
My light within always shines
I am driven to it
I always follow the signs

Fuller Inspirations

DAY 100

I've come a long way
I like the progress I've made
Change is inevitable
I make sure growth is displayed

Fuller Inspirations

DAY 101

I am responsible for my happiness
I shift all my thoughts higher
My mood follows closely behind
Peace and love is what I acquire

Fuller Inspirations

DAY 102

I seek knowledge daily
I expand my mind from reading
I spend time with thinkers
We all move forward and are leading

Fuller Inspirations

DAY 103

I use this time to flourish
I block interruptions and get centered
I set my alarm for this time daily
A state of peace, I have entered

Fuller Inspirations

DAY 104

I move Now on my ideas
I follow thru with each step
I think it all the way out
Then I get started once I prep

Fuller Inspirations

DAY 105

I am intentional in my thinking
I keep my mind on the prize
I stay focused on my goal
The plan is to see my level rise

Fuller Inspirations

DAY 106

I dream big
Then I put it to pen and pad
I focus on winning
Therefore, the more wins I add

Fuller Inspirations

DAY 107

I improve the lives of others
I inspire them to look within
Change comes from the individual
Riches are found in women and men

Fuller Inspirations

DAY 108

I increase my daily intake
I engulf myself with positive things
I dismiss any room for failure
Abundance is what this life brings

Fuller Inspirations

DAY 109

I am excited about my day
I always reach for the sky
Each minute, I make a choice
I hold onto my Dreams and fly

Fuller Inspirations

DAY 110

I have the courage to be me
I say my thoughts out loud
Even with the fear of being wrong
I speak up anyway and stay proud

Fuller Inspirations

DAY 111

Hey Self
It will work, just trust me
I bring my vision to fruition
Life is more than what I see

Fuller Inspirations

DAY 112

I've made many mistakes
I've tried over and over again
I persevere thru the hard times
That drives helps me win

Fuller Inspirations

DAY 113

I reflect on my life
All is as it should be
I accept the sum of my experiences
My actions enhance what is for me

Fuller Inspiration

DAY 114

I take time to rest
I deserve a moment to rejuvenate
I build my energy to move on
So that I may fulfill my Fate

Fuller Inspirations

DAY 115

I am Fearless
Yes, some doubts do live here
But I do it anyway
My VISION is bigger than my fear

Fuller Inspirations

DAY 116

I AM...
There are many possibilities
My life is what I make it
I create the life I want for me

Fuller Inspirations

DAY 117

I upgrade my life
I'm the only person who can
I improve myself daily
With consistency thru my lifespan

Fuller Inspirations

DAY 118

I am kind to myself
I understand if I make a wrong turn
I always build myself up
Knowing that from every action, I learn

Fuller Inspirations

DAY 119

I am mindful of my time
I make room for important task
I know how I'm spending this day
There is no question to even ask

Fuller Inspirations

DAY 120

I live this life for me
I focus on what I expect
Every life is different
All of who I am, I accept

Fuller Inspirations

DAY 121

I carefully choose how I speak
I know my words have power
Especially the words I say to me
"You're amazing!" like a florist to the flower

Fuller Inspirations

DAY 122

I attract Amazing people
They see the Joy in me
Together we emote happiness
Enough for the world to see

Fuller Inspirations

DAY 123

I am Thankful for all I have
All my needs are always met
I keep my eyes on the positive
Knowing that my world is my asset

Fuller Inspirations

DAY 124

I keep going
No matter what takes place
I finish what I start
Always getting back to home base

Fuller Inspirations

DAY 125

I am Confident
I release fear from my heart
I stand straight up
I know I'm the Best from the start

Fuller Inspirations

DAY 126

I have been thru this before
These type of obstacles I overcame
I know I can make it thru
"I am full of strength!" I proclaim

Fuller Inspirations

DAY 127

I am enjoying this life
I have fun with those around me
I take in each moment
And all the miracles that I see

Fuller Inspirations

DAY 128

I am Happy
Today is a great day
I am completing my to-do list
And finding joy in every way

Fuller Inspirations

DAY 129

I expect things to go right
If not, I know it's the plan
I never let it change how I think
I know I WILL because I can

Fuller Inspirations

DAY 130

I am Compassionate
I create a judgement free zone
Others feel at ease around me
I make people feel at home

Fuller Inspirations

DAY 131

I maintain positive relationships
Those that give love and support
I let go of negative people
I never compromise my comfort

Fuller Inspirations

DAY 132

I am ME
Even if I had a chance to choose
I am the BEST at doing me
Anyone who tries, will lose

Fuller Inspirations

DAY 133

I was born a Warrior
My actions maintain my position
I am BRAVE despite fear
I always accomplish my MISSION

Fuller Inspirations

DAY 134

I am WHOLE
Everything I need is in me
I am a MIRACLE walking
It's time I finally see

Fuller Inspirations

DAY 135

I do what I have to do
I do it until it's done
I accomplish all of my goals
All my challenges, I overcome

Fuller Inspirations

DAY 136

I stay committed to my goals
My persistence is the key
I continuously make progress
I always get where I need to be

Fuller Inspirations

DAY 137

I am THANKFUL
Each step, I celebrate
I am happy with my growth
I'm moving forward, I am Great

Fuller Inspirations

DAY 138

My heart forgives
I still see beauty on this day
I let go of the hurt
Faith helps me find the way

Fuller Inspirations

DAY 139

I improve my self talk
I always say, "I can!"
I prepare in advance
Growing is the master plan

Fuller Inspirations

DAY 140

I am PEACE
Speak slowly and say it again
I AM PEACE
I find my love and joy within

Fuller Inspirations

DAY 141

I see myself
I love who I truly am
I deserve this success
It's always been in my program

Fuller Inspirations

DAY 142

I rebuild my strength
I know life has ups and downs
I climb over this mountain
Getting my feet back to solid ground

Fuller Inspirations

DAY 143

I am Wealthy
I cherish my family and friends
I unconditionally love
It's the love that never ends

Fuller Inspirations

DAY 144

I am Better
Better than I was the day before
I intentionally grow
Putting my plan in action to soar

Fuller Inspirations

DAY 145

My mind is positive
I exercise it each day
I love LOVE
I bring kindness in every way

Fuller Inspirations

DAY 146

I live my dreams
Never following behind
I turn my hopes to action
Because of hard work, I shine

Fuller Inspirations

DAY 147

I live in harmony
My desires and needs are one
I make PEACE with myself
Everything falls into place when done

Fuller Inspirations

DAY 148

I dismiss all negativity
I let my voice within speak louder
I make a list of all my gifts
Knowing my worth, I feel PROUDER

Fuller Inspirations

DAY 149

I push aside all my worries
I find Peace in the present
I prepare for tomorrow
Not just wishing on a star and a crescent

Fuller Inspirations

DAY 150

I am a WINNER
No matter what you think, I've won
I continuously push my limits
Until I succeed, I'm never done

Fuller Inspirations

DAY 151

I always make it
Then I break at the finish line
I get back up
Then I do it again to beat my own time

Fuller Inspirations

DAY 152

I trust myself
My intuition never lies
No need to overthink it
My experiences make me wise

Fuller Inspirations

DAY 153

I am a person of integrity
My word, I always keep
I fulfill my commitments
And always speak with honesty

Fuller Inspirations

DAY 154

I am a patient person
Yet, I'm active at the same time
I know like I KNOW that it's coming
So I set up my life like it's already mine

Fuller Inspirations

DAY 155

My life is full of GREATNESS
I was born to make an impact
I keep my mind on the positive
The best of the best I attract

Fuller Inspirations

DAY 156

I accept life's struggles
I build skills from every trial
I make my situation even better
I stay optimistic, that's my style

Fuller Inspiration

DAY 157

I am a Treasure
I've searched high and low
I have the value in me
Now I know I have the Glow

Fuller Inspirations

DAY 158

I always Persevere
No matter how many doubts come my way
I keep going despite setbacks
I write out my plans every day

Fuller Inspirations

DAY 159

I am MINDFUL
I stay open to my present state
I am PURPOSEFUL in my thinking
Keeping my thoughts focused on this date

Fuller Inspirations

DAY 160

I am already connected to LOVE
Even having never physically met
You live in me and I in you
Fate predicts a meeting we will get

Fuller Inspirations

DAY 161

I trust my journey
Even the heartbreak was for me
I've grown and I've learned
I am at peace and I feel free

Fuller Inspirations

DAY 162

I can change the world
One good deed at a time
I embrace all humanity
I help my brothers and sisters climb

Fuller Inspirations

DAY 163

I love the work I do
I give my best on every project
I am proud of every outcome
Each day my to-do list gets checked

Fuller Inspirations

DAY 164

I always keep trying
I do better than I expect
My actions dictate my future
For every cause there's an effect

Fuller Inspiration

DAY 165

I speak powerful words
Especially the words I speak to me
I give myself love daily
My self talk lifts my positivity

Fuller Inspirations

DAY 166

I do the thing I fear most
That's the only way I conquer it
I challenge my Beliefs when they come
Thoughts become positive where I see fit

Fuller Inspirations

DAY 167

I stay grounded
I maintain a healthy balance
I am one with the earth
I release negative energy thru silence

Fuller Inspirations

DAY 168

Today, I will try something new
My results will be much better
I let go of complacency
I'm a certified go-getter

Fuller Inspirations

DAY 169

I always succeed
My determination never fades
My life experiences are my classroom
And I always get good grades

Fuller Inspirations

DAY 170

I have the answers within
I listen when there is silence
I block my mind from distractions
I pay attention to the guidance

Fuller Inspirations

DAY 171

I speak my mind
I always do it with respect
I not only try to be understood
I seek to understand so we can connect

Fuller Inspirations

DAY 172

I am the conductor of my emotions
I keep my perspective positive
I shield myself from the pessimists
Keeping my distance is my prerogative

Fuller Inspirations

DAY 173

I remove myself from the chaos
No need to acknowledge it with a speech
I humbly walk towards peace
That experience was there to teach

Fuller Inspirations

DAY 174

I step up with confidence
I speak clearly when I take the stage
I am comfortable in my own skin
Even if I feel no one is on the same page

Fuller Inspirations

DAY 175

I feel moved to do it
So, I'm moving and doing it
I am active towards my goal
I finish it and never quit

Fuller Inspirations

DAY 176

I'm committed to growing
I take in the wisdom around me
I ask questions when needed
Following my FAITH completely

Fuller Inspirations

DAY 177

I Encourage myself
I uplift my inner child
I heal from past pain
Always making myself smile

Fuller Inspirations

DAY 178

I put my focus on my wants
I know they will arrive
I let go of disappointment
I make my dreams come alive

Fuller Inspirations

DAY 179

I am DILIGENT in completing task
I predict my next phase
I have no choice but to move forward
My level rises always

Fuller Inspirations

DAY 180

I let go of shame
Knowing my biggest critic is me
I forgive myself for any mistakes
That's the only way I'll be free

Fuller Inspirations

DAY 181

I only focus on the end game
Obstacles build my tenacity
I become stronger and wiser
Only to expand my capacity

Fuller Inspirations

DAY 182

I show not tell
My dreams are bigger than what I say
I believe in me
But showing action with belief is the way

Fuller Inspirations

DAY 183

My reflection is my perception
I have learned to accept me
Inner Peace I have found
In the mirror, I LOVE what I see

Fuller Inspirations

DAY 184

I do what I have to do
Even when the motivation subsides
I am great at keeping my plans
I am where work and consistency collides

Fuller Inspirations

DAY 185

I offer kindness to the universe
I am surrounded by friends and family
We harmoniously work together
There is peace all around me

Fuller Inspirations

DAY 186

I am pleased to meet new people
Their stories often connect us
I make room for expansion
Growth in my relationships is a plus

Fuller Inspirations

DAY 187

I have creative ideas
I make moves to see them thru
I am PROUD of the path I've chosen
I release fear when starting anew

Fuller Inspirations

DAY 188

I have perfect health
I accept my body as a whole
I love all of these parts
Loving myself, fills my soul

Fuller Inspirations

DAY 189

I make smart decisions
I seek wisdom from around me
I learn from my errors
And keep going indefinitely

Fuller Inspirations

DAY 190

I keep silent when needed
I always give time to think things thru
I gain all the information
Proceeding with respect at each rendez-vous

Fuller Inspirations

DAY 191

I treat my neighbors with love
Even when I don't feel my best
I see the beauty in everyone
I approach the world with zest

Fuller Inspirations

DAY 192

I am GRATEFUL for my life
I appreciate each day
I carry my object of gratitude
Remembering my blessings along the way

Fuller Inspirations

DAY 193

I am in tune with my skills
I enhance on what I need to know
I take time to develop my craft
I plant seeds so they will sow

Fuller Inspirations

DAY 194

I am truly one of a kind
My differences set me apart
But we are more alike than not
We are connected at the heart

Fuller Inspirations

DAY 195

I continue on this journey
Knowing that the rewards do arrive
I am a flower pushing thru the surface
My roots grow first, then I thrive

Fuller Inspirations

DAY 196

I am open to new things
I release anxiety of the unknown
I commit myself to trying
While staying in a positive zone

Fuller Inspirations

DAY 197

I focus on what I can control
And watch everything else get aligned
I feel happy everyday
Completing the goals I have outlined

Fuller Inspirations

DAY 198

Good morning life
I am your pilot for today
The wind is calm and peaceful
My thoughts are positive in every way

Fuller Inspirations

DAY 199

I maintain my persistence
Even if I stumble along the way
I am focused on the end result
It's about how I finish my day

Fuller Inspirations

DAY 200

I embrace all challenges
They make me a stronger me
I get better with time
I face any difficulty

Fuller Inspirations

DAY 201

I am stronger due to my experiences
Even if I once wished they didn't occur
I know my path has purpose
Getting thru each trial, I am happier

Fuller Inspirations

DAY 202

I always get to the finish line
Even if I had to cry thru the pain
I see my endurance as a reward
Stopping once doesn't prevent the gain

Fuller Inspirations

DAY 203

I have the confidence of a child
Obstacles don't really exist
When I want the rewards on the top shelf
No worries, I'll get them-I insist

Fuller Inspirations

DAY 204

I control how I react
Knowing that situations still come
The impact no longer phases me
I only march to my drum

Fuller Inspirations

DAY 205

Anything I start
I always finish
Any surfacing doubt
I quickly diminish

Fuller Inspirations

DAY 206

Thank you for the wisdom
And the ability to discern
I gain from all my experiences
I am always seeking to learn

Fuller Inspirations

DAY 207

I choose to have Faith
Fear never got me anywhere
I believe in the unseen
The same way I breathe in air

Fuller Inspirations

DAY 208

I see things clearly
I have everything I need
My faith lives in me
I nurture it like watering a seed

Fuller Inspirations

DAY 209

I am the author of this story
I write out my life each day
I am living my life on purpose
Fulfilling my FATE in every way

Fuller Inspirations

DAY 210

I welcome the uncertainty
I take risk so I can grow
Challenges make me stronger
This for certain, I know

Fuller Inspirations

DAY 211

I have Love within me
No need to seek it from outside
I already possess the answer
I follow my inner guide

Fuller Inspirations

DAY 212

I am ready for the Glow-Up
I have prepared for this
I put in all the hard work
And put checks down the list

Fuller Inspirations

DAY 213

My yesterday can predict my tomorrow
I make the most of my actions today
I choose to improve myself always
I watch my thoughts and what I say

Fuller Inspirations

DAY 214

I always aim high
No need to settle for less
I turn my vision into reality
Watch me as I progress

Fuller Inspirations

DAY 215

I am currently getting it done
Even if I have no clue how
I work step by step on my goal
To win in this life is my vow

Fuller Inspirations

DAY 216

I stop and look around
I am GRATEFUL for this day
In this moment I am happy
I find PEACE in every way

Fuller Inspirations

DAY 217

I am a Unique individual
It's okay if I go against the grain
I love myself for who I am
And I'm okay being in my own lane

Fuller Inspirations

DAY 218

I've made it this far
I release any doubt and fear
I keep pushing towards my goals
After this the next is near

Fuller Inspirations

DAY 219

I always make the Best choice
Whether my decision is wrong or right
They say you win some or you learn
Either way I gain wisdom and insight

Fuller Inspirations

DAY 220

I maintain self control
When I know that it's not for me
I sit comfortably with my choices
Fulfilling my Destiny is a guarantee

Fuller Inspirations

DAY 221

I embrace having dreams
Knowing I have to do the work too
The more dreams the better
I keep abundance flowing thru

Fuller Inspirations

DAY 222

I always continue on
Even when the road seems long
I overcome any personal battles
Even if I shed a tear, I'm still strong

Fuller Inspirations

DAY 223

I have a different vision
Despite us looking at the same thing
I see opportunity when you see hardships
The morning alarm is even a good ring

Fuller Inspirations

DAY 224

I increase my attempts
Despite failure being an option
I become an expert at my craft
Taking all the necessary action

Fuller Inspirations

DAY 225

I love Me forever
I love My future and My past
Mostly, I love Me on this day
It's the kind of love that last

Fuller Inspirations

DAY 226

I stay ready
Where opportunity and preparation meet
I practice despite a booking
My determination makes you take a seat

Fuller Inspirations

DAY 227

I am BOLD
Bold enough to express how I feel
It's okay to be vulnerable
Owning my feelings is keeping it real

Fuller Inspirations

DAY 228

I am ABLE
Even when others counted me out
I reach past any limit
Breaking barriers is what I'm about

Fuller Inspirations

DAY 229

I breathe in PEACE
And then I relax my face
I release stress from my shoulders
I stay aware of my current space

Fuller Inspirations

DAY 230

My growth is inevitable
I learn something new everyday
I create endless options
I work first then I play

Fuller Inspirations

DAY 231

I am PROUD of me
I work hard to finish my goal
I applaud even the little steps
My tenacity makes me feel whole

Fuller Inspirations

DAY 232

I audaciously get to my purpose
Continuous moves clear my path
I have more losses than wins
But the wins weigh more do the math

Fuller Inspirations

DAY 233

My voice is powerful
Even when I speak softly
I embody confidence and love
I inspire those around me

Fuller Inspirations

DAY 234

I am ALIVE
Living to present the best me
I feel GRATEFUL for each breath
I am who I choose to be

Fuller Inspirations

DAY 235

I ADORE me
I hold myself in high regard
My light shines from within
I am a walking greeting card

Fuller Inspirations

DAY 236

I feel APPRECIATED
Even if the words don't always come
My reward comes from within
I wake up feeling like I've won

Fuller Inspirations

DAY 237

I am BRILLIANT
I study the lessons of my choice
I seek knowledge on the daily
It builds confidence in my voice

Fuller Inspirations

DAY 238

I clear space for positive vibes
I only let in the GOOD
I am kind to those around me
Giving generosity is understood

Fuller Inspirations

DAY 239

I am DYNAMIC
Positive energy flows my way
I work at being a better person
I treat today like it's my birthday

Fuller Inspirations

DAY 240

I am EMPOWERED
By the journey of my Ancestors
I stand tall on their achievements
For this life, they are my investors

Fuller Inspirations

DAY 241

I am comfortable asking for help
I know I have room to grow
It is an ingredient to success
Adding it all to what I know

Fuller Inspirations

DAY 242

I challenge myself
I break free from my comfort zone
I am able to take on any adventure
Even if it means sometimes I'm alone

Fuller Inspirations

DAY 243

I am Passionate about my life
It is the best gift of all
I make purposeful choices
So that I'm ready for the call

Fuller Inspirations

DAY 244

I play the leading role
I am the star of my life
I get awards and accolades
They come from my inner light

Fuller Inspirations

DAY 245

I am Relentless
Despite any push back
I stay in the zone
I move forward on this track

Fuller Inspirations

DAY 246

I know what makes me happy
I start my morning that way
It sets the tone for each step
I am happy and vibrant today

Fuller Inspirations

DAY 247

I start where I am
Catching up only to me
I am happy with my progress
I make moves consistently

Fuller Inspirations

DAY 248

I nurture my dream
I feed it A PLAN then ACTION
I am Optimistic about growth
So I show it LOVE and AFFECTION

Fuller Inspirations

DAY 249

I am healed from the pain
They say it gets better with time
I accept my life as it is
It really all starts with the mind

Fuller Inspirations

DAY 250

I deserve it
All the good that comes my way
I am overwhelmingly Grateful
I stay in tune to my Blessings today

Fuller Inspirations

DAY 251

I adapt to change
Knowing that's fate taking the wheel
I adjust to my new reality
Learning to persevere is a skill

Fuller Inspirations

DAY 252

I set my mind to it
I get what I desire
I feel it in my spirit
I am building my Empire

Fuller Inspirations

DAY 253

I take care of me
Then I can give to others
It refuels my energy
So I can help my sisters and brothers

Fuller Inspirations

DAY 254

I am talented
And I still outwork the next
I make sure I'm the last one standing
My perseverance is how I flex

Fuller Inspirations

DAY 255

I am Grounded
I am present for what's around me
I Welcome life as it is
I feel safe and protected for eternity

Fuller Inspirations

DAY 256

I work on my goals everyday
So that the should-ofs don't exist
I make my life how I want it
Even if trials come, I persist

Fuller Inspirations

DAY 257

I am Compassionate
I help others in need
I seek to remove burdens
Always acting with speed

Fuller Inspirations

DAY 258

I am emotionally fulfilled
I shower myself with love everyday
I am connected to my peace
It magnetizes others towards my way

Fuller Inspirations

DAY 259

I am BRAVE
I step out and try new things
I let go of the fear
My FAITH expands my wings

Fuller Inspirations

DAY 260

I plant seeds of success
Everything I touch turns to gold
Trust me, I'm working for it
I stay consistent and never fold

Fuller Inspirations

DAY 261

I am Prosperous
I am flourishing from the inside out
I have a can-do attitude
I release negativity and doubt

Fuller Inspirations

DAY 262

I am accepting of compliments
And I give them just the same
I say Thank you with no explanation
Feeling proud is my aim

Fuller Inspirations

DAY 263

I am relaxed everyday
I choose to be worry free
Because I Prayed on the matter
I've learned to let it be

Fuller Inspirations

DAY 264

My inner child deserves the world
And I am definitely going to get it
I am accomplishing all my goals
Providing the best life I see fit

Fuller Inspirations

DAY 265

I am flexible
I know plans do change
I make room for the unexpected
I'm okay with the need to rearrange

Fuller Inspirations

DAY 266

I accept myself
I consciously remove the mask
I am free to be me
Understanding myself is the first task

Fuller Inspirations

DAY 267

I surrender to my divine path
And I feel amazingly free
My mind is now clearer
I see things I could not see

Fuller Inspirations

DAY 268

I am Fantastic
I don't need any explanation
I tell myself, "Get up and do it!"
I make moves without hesitation

Fuller Inspirations

DAY 269

I wear my Crown
Even when it feels like it's heavy
I am a servant to mankind
Royalty always stays ready

Fuller Inspirations

DAY 270

I am Successful
I keep going until the end
I stay laser beam focused
I have no choice but to win

Fuller Inspirations

DAY 271

I've seen this before
Winning is not new to me
I visualize my success
I excel, it's my Destiny

Fuller Inspirations

DAY 272

The rain will stop
So I'm proceeding with my plans
I am always Ambitious
My future is in my hands

Fuller Inspirations

DAY 273

I am Likeable
I show up as the Authentic me
People respect what's genuine
My true colors they always see

Fuller Inspirations

DAY 274

I am Happy with me
No one else can walk in my shoes
I accept my imperfections
I am my own Muse

Fuller Inspirations

DAY 275

I am Adventurous
It's the experiences that I live for
I am open to new ideas
And I always strive for more

Fuller Inspirations

DAY 276

I have a Wonderful life
Leaving behind all the What-ifs
Everything happens for a reason
I know all my experiences are gifts

Fuller Inspirations

DAY 277

I am happy giving to others
And I expect nothing in return
My rewards come from a higher source
This is a lesson I have learned

Fuller Inspirations

DAY 278

I maintain my discipline
So that I rise to the next level
I get done what needs to get done
Fear thinks I'm a rebel

Fuller Inspirations

DAY 279

I am sure of my choice
I stand on solid ground
I proceed with confidence
All of my decisions are sound

Fuller Inspirations

DAY 280

I embrace the entire moment
Giving my all to the cause
I am aware of things I can control
I keep going and give myself applause

Fuller Inspirations

DAY 281

I am committed to my Purpose
It is my Why that drives me
I keep going even if I don't feel it
The end result I clearly see

Fuller Inspirations

DAY 282

I am excited about my life
I expect things to be Great
I move like I own the world
Happiness is my Fate

Fuller Inspirations

DAY 283

I improve myself
Even when I wish the struggle was easy
I have the skills that I need
I continuously get better, believe me

Fuller Inspirations

DAY 284

I am Resilient
I bounce back from the pain
I always come out on top
Even my downfalls help me gain

Fuller Inspirations

DAY 285

I am aware of the Big Picture
Knowing this setback doesn't define me
I am Greater than this moment
The plan is always to shine victoriously

Fuller Inspirations

DAY 286

I take three deep breaths
While I close my eyes
I am the Master of my Destiny
I get all that I visualize

Fuller Inspirations

DAY 287

I always stand out
Fitting in, dulls my shine
I am an Outstanding person
I face the world and get what's mine

Fuller Inspirations

DAY 288

I've reached my moment of clarity
I know what it is I am to do
I am Overwhelmed with Joy
The answer, I already knew

Fuller Inspirations

DAY 289

I might not know what I'm doing
I still put one foot in front of the other
I stay open to the answers
When listening, the truth, I uncover

Fuller Inspirations

DAY 290

I continuously make progress
Therefore, Winning is my only choice
I am Optimistic about what's next
For every increase, I rejoice

Fuller Inspirations

DAY 291

I awaken to a rebirth
Every day begins a new journey
I am confident in my choices
I take action to get what's for me

Fuller Inspirations

DAY 292

I always search within
I AM what makes me Whole
I am connected to my Higher Source
That's the only way I GROW

Fuller Inspirations

DAY 293

Hey, it's okay to start over
I now see my path clearly
I am persistent with my goal
Consider it done, Sincerely

Fuller Inspirations

DAY 294

I maintain self control
Even when my emotions are on fire
My Calmness is my Strength
And my Spirituality lifts me higher

Fuller Inspirations

DAY 295

I keep pushing
Impossible things do come true
I am Tenacious in my drive
Despite the obstacle, I make it thru

Fuller Inspirations

DAY 296

I am Love
Filled with Joy and Gratitude
I show Kindness to everyone
Love is an Action not just a mood

Fuller Inspirations

DAY 297

I am Grateful in advance
I create the magic I want in my life
I am Joyful because of my plans
My happiness brings out my inner light

Fuller Inspirations

DAY 298

I believe everything happens for a reason
So I never really sweat the small things
I have an Optimistic attitude
I handle business like Queens and Kings

Fuller Inspirations

DAY 299

I accept all of my experiences
None of us are above the trials
I continuously learn and grow
Storing the lessons in my files

Fuller Inspirations

DAY 300

I Believe in me
Just as I believe in you
I know I can do anything
This, I hold to be true

Fuller Inspirations

DAY 301

I am one with the flow
Staying aligned with the divine order
I listen to my inner voice
My purpose stretches beyond my border

Fuller Inspirations

DAY 302

I am always changing
Which means I'm moving too
I choose the direction I move in
Even if sometimes I have to push thru

Fuller Inspirations

DAY 303

I am so happy
I feel it in all that is me
I've been planning for this win
Now it's time for others to see

Fuller Inspirations

DAY 304

I see Greatness in my life
My vision is bigger than my reality
But my work ethic matches my vision
So my dream is my real life in actuality

Fuller Inspirations

DAY 305

I keep my actions the same
Even when the hurt dwells in me
I know this too will pass
I always continue to be friendly

Fuller Inspirations

DAY 306

I am Happy now
Rather than waiting on something new
I make the changes happen
And when more comes, I'm Grateful too

Fuller Inspirations

DAY 307

I accept the past as it is
Knowing that no one owes me anything
I get my gifts from above
And I receive Peace and many Blessings

Fuller Inspirations

DAY 308

I encourage myself
And leave the "about tos" behind
I do what I can do today
And claim all that is mine

Fuller Inspirations

DAY 309

I am Aware of who I am
I sit and reflect on my days
I am happy being me
I love all of my ways

Fuller Inspirations

DAY 310

I free my mind
I release myself from limits
I stay focused on the positives
Negative thoughts, I prohibit

Fuller Inspirations

DAY 311

I let go of old patterns
So I can make space for the new
I embrace my next level
And show gratitude because I grew

Fuller Inspirations

DAY 312

I continue to go the distance
I put one foot in front of the next
I am destined to reach my goal
It's the power of cause and effect

Fuller Inspirations

DAY 313

I know this experience is just a chapter
The story of my life turns out GREAT
I can get thru any and every trial
To experience joy, I need not wait

Fuller Inspirations

DAY 314

I remove the hurdles created by doubt
I stay Faithful that my dreams come true
I handle my business like a Pro
Before it happened, I already knew

Fuller Inspirations

DAY 315

I live my life on purpose
And I do it with excitement
My Purpose is what drives me
Faith brings me enlightenment

Fuller Inspirations

DAY 316

I have magic in my steps
When I move, the path is created
I am guided by my vision
Reaching my goal, I am elated

Fuller Inspirations

DAY 317

Today I'm getting up
I'm doing that thing on the list
I'm writing out all the steps
I am an Achiever who persists

Fuller Inspirations

DAY 318

I know pain sometimes comes
I keep my attitude positive
Things always seem to work out
Optimistic is my defining adjective

Fuller Inspirations

DAY 319

I relish in each moment
Time is my friend
I enjoy it ALL in the now
I close my eyes and breathe in

Fuller Inspirations

DAY 320

I am inspired to follow my purpose
My Why continuously calls me
I plan it out and act on my dreams
I have Faith that it is my reality

Fuller Inspirations

DAY 321

I am Happy for my Success
I worked hard for this
I stay focused on the end result
So, my Goal, I never miss

Fuller Inspirations

DAY 322

I take time to interrupt my patterns
So I can think about my progress
I make changes in my life where needed
I want better not just familiar I confess

Fuller Inspirations

DAY 323

I am one with the Earth
I spend time with Nature
I feel protected everyday
I study Peace, it's my major

Fuller Inspirations

DAY 324

I trust my process
I feel confident on my path
Everything happens for a reason
I know it's working on my behalf

Fuller Inspirations

DAY 325

I accept myself
Loving my flaws and ALL
I am Worthy as I am
Self love is the protocol

Fuller Inspirations

DAY 326

I make it a habit to progress
I show up everyday
My will power is consistent
Getting it done is my pay

Fuller Inspirations

DAY 327

I am creative
I sit in silence to hear my mind
I let go of distractions
My self expression is not confined

Fuller Inspirations

DAY 328

I honor my calling
I stay immersed in my passion
I learn the skills that are needed
My knowledge is my fashion

Fuller Inspirations

DAY 329

I am a person of strength
My strength has been put to the test
I rise to any challenge
I succeed because I'm the best

Fuller Inspirations

DAY 330

I upgrade my life
I'm the only one who can
I start on my inner self
Loving me is where I began

Fuller Inspirations

DAY 331

I am happy helping others
Not just because I got it like that
I am a humble helper
One day I might need it right back

Fuller Inspirations

DAY 332

I enjoy the simple things
I take time to smell the flowers
I am uplifted by the sunrise
I listen to the wind blow for hours

Fuller Inspirations

DAY 333

I am kindness and compassion
I am what lies beneath
I am patience and perseverance
I am more than what you see

Fuller Inspirations

DAY 334

I accept the closing of this chapter
I welcome my new beginning
I am Appreciative of my journey
With every step, I am winning

Fuller Inspirations

DAY 335

I have the "Je ne sais quoi"
They can't quite put it into words
I have GREATNESS in my Essence
I am soaring higher than the birds

Fuller Inspirations

DAY 336

I am rebuilding my life
Now it's on solid foundation
I Love myself
It's time I get in Formation

Fuller Inspirations

DAY 337

Dear Comfort Zone
We're over and thru
I challenge myself
Those fears are not true

Fuller Inspirations

DAY 338

I Empower myself
I live up to my expectations
I complete all my goals
I stick it out thru the duration

Fuller Inspirations

DAY 339

I am Free to make tough decisions
Some doors, I have to close
I realize they take me to a dead end
Knowing when to let go, one grows

Fuller Inspirations

DAY 340

I am Powerful
I turn a maybe into a must
I make obstacles seem small
Trust me, I always adjust

Fuller Inspirations

DAY 341

I am ready when it comes
Success is part of the agenda
This is more than some luck
It's hard work in all its splendor

Fuller Inspirations

DAY 342

I always improve
Even if it's a little at a time
I am GRATEFUL for the small steps
My perseverance helps me climb

Fuller Inspirations

DAY 343

I am Amazed at myself
I push my fear to the side
I did that thing anyway
I meet my goals and build my Pride

Fuller Inspirations

DAY 344

I keep my same Energy
Even if I failed the last time
I know I can do it
My motivation stays at its prime

Fuller Inspirations

DAY 345

I welcome the unknown
Learning is so Exciting
I am Brave enough to try
My attitude is inviting

Fuller Inspirations

DAY 346

I work well with others
Together we accomplish more
I share and accept new ideas
Networking always opens the door

Fuller Inspirations

DAY 347

I am Courageous
Courageous enough to be me
I live each day to the fullest
Living in my truth and being free

Fuller Inspirations

DAY 348

I am Dedicated
I plan for the life I want
I keep going despite fear
My mission stays in the forefront

Fuller Inspirations

DAY 349

I stay focused on ONE thing
I give it my all until it's complete
I become an Expert at it
My follow-thru makes me Elite

Fuller Inspirations

DAY 350

I continue to Win
I make sacrifices for my Dream
I move everything out of my way
I stay amongst the Best Team

Fuller Inspirations

DAY 351

I am a Generous person
Giving to others heals my soul
I share more than just things
Connecting to others makes me Whole

Fuller Inspirations

DAY 352

I am destined to Succeed
I'm more afraid of not trying
I accept a fail as it comes
Winning is then more gratifying

Fuller Inspirations

DAY 353

I push myself to the next phase
Then I reward all my progress
I take each lesson with me
Learning is part of the process

Fuller Inspirations

DAY 354

I am Healing
And every thought is with intent
I take time to listen
Releasing toxins with my consent

Fuller Inspirations

DAY 355

I communicate with compassion
Even my truth is peaceful and kind
I consider others' feelings
The way I want them to care for mine

Fuller Inspirations

DAY 356

I continuously make progress
With a few sacrifices along the way
I always reach my goal
I grow and flourish come what may

Fuller Inspirations

DAY 357

I am at home within myself
I accept me for all that I am
I have found what I was seeking
I finally passed my own exam

Fuller Inspirations

DAY 358

I have infinite possibilities
I live my dreams every day
I always take the bet
I dare to make my own way

Fuller Inspirations

DAY 359

I make time for my challenges
I face the fear and do it anyway
It's the only way that I grow
And I'm also thriving I must say

Fuller Inspirations

DAY 360

I believe in me
I'm the only cheerleader I need
My confidence has no doubts
Because I've been planted the seed

Fuller Inspirations

DAY 361

I run this life
I own my next 24
I do what I want
I'm kicking in the door

Fuller Inspirations

DAY 362

I let go of the need for control
What's meant to be, will always be
I am able to see things more clearly
And put my energy into what's for me

Fuller Inspirations

DAY 363

I embrace life's challenges
I know they only elevate my score
I like how my level rises
Each experience helps me grow more

Fuller Inspirations

DAY 364

I am Extraordinary
Because I work while you sleep
I do more than I did yesterday
My actions cause a quantum leap

Fuller Inspirations

DAY 365

Thank you for all the good times
Thank you for the times that were not so right
Thank you for the lessons that come with them
Thank you for giving me vision and not just sight

Fuller Inspirations

Made in the USA
Las Vegas, NV
21 June 2022